Scientific Prospectus on Star Fleet

Miguel A. Sanchez-Rey

Table Contents

The Beginning of Star Fleet

The Star Fleet Protocol

Star Fleet Regulations

Star Fleet Command

The Star Fleet Primary Directive

Log

Appendix: Star Trek is War-Like

The Beginning of Star Fleet

The Leading Professor Miguel Angel Sanchez-Rey [*The Grandmaster, The Master of Space-Time*]

The Academy of Advance Science and the Technological Sciences

With PHPR [The Physicalist Program], the stage is set to overhaul the entire notion of what is understood as the merit system. In that way, the AASTS [The Academy of Advance Science and the Technological Sciences] was founded as a crisis control measure after the academic hierarchy collapse with the permanent decline of the religious state. Leading to the founding of utopian science as the next step in the political sciences.

By fully implementing PHPR, gradually will the planet begin to slip into a quiet and serene state (where a 40-year window of opportunity is giving to stand down military hostilities amongst the major superpowers). After which The First Task is to be slowly and carefully completed. Marking a 100-year task in which the planet will go through increasing bouts of celebration.

The Second Task has been establish as the resolution to an extraterrestrial conflict. Whereby the aim is to achieve the internationalist model by searching out for habitable zones, through peaceful First Contact, in an attempt to safely expand from Earth's solar

system. And to begin the transition of phasing out the planetary super-

state. Which will lead to the achievement of a healthy and vibrant

Anarcho-syndicalist society in the form of a federation of democratic

industries (under the stipulation of the internationalist model).

Approximately a century before arriving at Class 2, in the Omega-

Kardeshev scale, where humanity achieves the harnessing of a star.

With that in mind, PHPR and the AASTS will culminate with the

founding of a global military defense. A global military defense task in

promoting scientific exploration and imposing self-defense from any

internal/external threat to the planetary super-state. A military defense

force that will reshape the merit system -- in terms, of achieving and

sustaining academic harmony rather than hierarchy.

In that manner, the global military defense will not intervene in the

affairs of civil society but instead all knowledge of space exploration,

until a certain point, is to be kept away from the civil population. Least cry havoc and quiet mayhem is to be unleashed on a planetary scale that may jeopardize the council of the scientific planetary super-state (that is to take unilateral and authoritative action to protect the planetary super-state and the democratic workforce).

Merit and achievement is to be the bases of preserving a harmonic stage in human intellectual development. Where a healthy sense of cooperation and competition (like the interplay of multiple methodologies of competing strategies) coincides with devoting oneself to the preservation of what's left of the religious state. Whereby one does not declare a fanatical allegiance to the super-state, rather in defending tranquility and sustaining some measure of peace-time.

As the beginning of Star Fleet means that a heavy burden is to be bestow -- to those who enlist for the sake of scientific exploration and planetary military defense. So as not to cause the toppling of the planetary super-state (consequentially exacerbating collective psychosis).

For those reasons merit and achievement means that the prize system is to await orders, and not to interfere in the affairs of the super-state, but to reward on the bases of outcome rather than promise and/or potentiality. And that to those who are awarded merit and achievement (basing their merit and achievement on outcome) is to retire from public service and allow others to take on the role of preserving global scientific harmony.

The AASTS is to take leadership position when top-level decision-making and leadership fails. PHPR is design as the resolution to a foreseeable catastrophic scenario in the Scientific Age in the form of a task. PHPR is to be dismantled when the last task is completed. By then the Scientific Age has come to an end. So that one regains open public participation in the sciences -- where the boundaries of the prize system, doctoral system, and ranking system is no longer blurred.

The AASTS is to lead the way to the incalculable technological stage (and by then fully dismantled). And open access no longer leads to cry havoc or quiet mayhem -- cause by unstable decision-making, that could destabilize the scientific process. Potentially leading to mutiny, i.e., the doctoral system is to be dismantled at the dawn of the Advance Age.

That is the essence of the other task of PHPR, understood as perpetual anticipatory economics, which will preserve the federation of democratic industrial economies while dismantling the planetary super-state -- in hopes of self-actualizing the internationalist model on an intergalactic scale. Where the planetary biosphere will slip into a dream-like state, and peace-time is preserved, until the incalculable technological stage is reach. Such that all current notions of scientific historical materialism completely breakdown.

Star Fleet Protocol

Star Fleet orders are to protect and/or defend the planetary super-state, and the habitable zones, from any internal and/or external threat…

To explore charted and uncharted space to further space exploration, scientific discovery and peaceful co-existence...

To obey the primary Star Fleet Directive…

Star Fleet is to be dismantled when peace-time is extended indefinitely…

Star Fleet Regulations

Star Fleet regulations dictates that commanding officers are to obey orders at all cost. To follow Star Fleet directives accordingly and not to disobey the chain of command. Star Fleet regulations states that officers are to graduate from their prospective war colleges if they are to join Star Fleet and eventually take command of Star Fleet Protocol.

Regulations are to be put in place to guide Star Fleet in realizing protocol. But regulations are neither to cause harm nor pain to others but to achieve Star Fleet's enduring mission to defend tranquility and sustain peace-time. And that any corroborated violation of regulations be met with swift action against the violators if not to be dismissed from Star Fleet.

Star Fleet Command

Star Fleet Command is base on various planetary locations on the habitable zones. They guide and give orders to Star Fleet vessels that travel in and out of the habitable zones while also refraining from entering the outer habitable zones. Star Fleet command also communicates with nearly 40-intelligent species but no direct contact is made since co-habitation (due to biological differences) can be made and in which these species choose to remain neutral from human political and social affairs. Star Fleet Command is where the Star Fleet Council is also situated and in which they set the fleet's mission and directives.

For Star Fleet Command objective is to protect the habitable zones and to lay claim to new habitable zones upon approval through safe first contact. Without interfering in the affairs of the outer habitable zones that lay new worlds that are not to be explored or interfered in least conflict should be instigated or unleash on an interplanetary scale.

Star Fleet Command aims to bring peace-time to the habitable zones and to extend peace-time by promoting unity and the federalist principle of the internationalist model.

The Star Fleet Primary Directive

The Star Fleet primary directive is to refrain from communicating and/or encroaching on any other intelligent life-forms unless Star Fleet Command gives approval that such communication or interaction be deemed necessary and/or imperative to Star Fleet Protocol. That no First Contact is to be attempted unless Star Fleet Command gives direct orders that such First Contact is to be initiated on the grounds of existentiality. For conflict is to be avoided at all cost with any other intelligent life-forms.

Star Fleet has every right to defend the interest of the internationalist model. To use unilateral decision-making to decide the peaceful fate of many planets and their inhabitants that agree to adhere to such model. A fleet that numbers in the millions. That travels in and out of star gates and worm-holes.

Utilizing cryogenics and genetic enhancements to extend human life in space. While applying advance consciousness to achieve a collective interface, that will allow Star Fleet to keep in close contact with their vessels and space-habitats (while their officers and astronauts keep in close contact with each other through perpetual existence).

Even though life is plentiful there can be no cohabitation. And even though most intelligent life chose to refrain from direct long-term contact a vibrant economic and/or political model has been set that has kept Star Fleet from succumbing to war-time. A wildly strong predisposition is engrained in Star Fleet's protocols and expansion that yields new entrees into the internationalist model, on the bases of free markets, is a vital aspect of securing peace-time and yielding advances in the sciences and space exploration.

With that in mind, Star Fleet will continue its mission to further the internationalist model and to preserve unanimity amongst all alien races.

Appendix

Star Trek is War-Like

[Author: Miguel A. Sanchez-Rey]

Star Trek is a science-fiction genre set in the distant future, around the 22nd to 24th century, that takes astronauts on an exploration mission across many planets that addresses problems that are metamorphic to the historical consciousness of the mid-20th and early early-21th century. Utilizing science-related themes with highly speculative technological ideas, that help to carry out the many stories of the Star Trek universe, would-be astronauts enlist in Star Fleet under the leadership of the United Federation of Planets headquarter on planet Earth.

The United Federation of Planets was founded to unite the known planets, capable of warp-drive, that came into first contact in earlier era of the star trek universe. That by the prime directive only planets capable of warp-drive are qualified to make first contact with Star Fleet.

Conflict in Star Trek subsume the majority of the plots in the star trek universe. Conflict with alien intelligences that ravishes the star trek universe. For example: the Klingons relationship with the United Federation of Planets has been relatively unstable up to the present and the Borg has been an existential threat to the Star Trek universe without end.

The star trek genre thrives in the idea of conflict. While it also addresses social and technological problems without embedding conflict into the star trek universe there is no entertainment value to the star trek universe. As to motivate the star trek universe requires the idea that war is good and peace is bad. War is good because it sustains a war-like society that thrives in conflict. Peace is bad because no purpose is to be gain from a highly-technological sedentary society. The interplay between conflict and self-actualization is at the heart of the Star Trek universe. But one can be misled to believe that what appears to be an innocent interplay between self-actualization and conflict, as James T. Kirk's self-realization as the captain of the U.S.S. Enterprise or Data's desire to be more human, in the Star Trek Generation genre, is in actual a prelude to war-crime. As to achieve self-actualization and to reach the climax of the star trek story war-crime must be committed on a large-scale to prove a point. A point that without conflict; without pain and grief, there can be no self-actualization and yet to self-actualize in star trek requires, in most cases, a large-scale conflict that unleashes havoc to planet Earth and all other alien worlds. That to reach the peak of self-actualization the star trek universe must undergo the grief of the death of countless many that number at a death-toll proportional to that of a giant Earth-like planet.

Even then star trek's desire for exploration has skewed the boundaries that limit encroaching into other solar habitats or other alien occupied regional systems. Encroaching into alien worlds sets the stage for a massive conflict and propels the story of the star trek universe. As the captain of the enterprise must constantly make two crucial choices: avoid conflict or take action? Obey Star-Fleet command or disobey? That is whether or not the captain of Enterprise is willing to be implicated in war-crime and face the dire consequences that amount to nothing, no less and no more, than the false realization of self-actualization in which in truth the captain should be brought up on charges and face harsh prosecution in the Federation Council.

The unstable nature of the star trek universe makes the plot and stories of star trek suspect. Even though it satisfies one's desire to see the transitional future it nevertheless is a genre of metaphor that relates to present-day historical trauma's and ordeals. Though it reveals ideas with strong liberal themes it nevertheless mixes them with the concept of the antagonist and protagonist element of the modern film plot. That is to say the one is not dealing with an innocent genre of would-be astronauts that strive to self-actualize and reach for the stars by addressing modern social and political themes but the willingness to take part in conflict, on both a local and galactic level, to achieve a sense of fulfillment while ignoring and skewing the reality of the death of hundreds, thousands and millions that would inevitably land the captain of the enterprise in a war-crime tribunal either on planet Earth or in an alien planet facing life-in-prison or execution for ignoring orders from Star Fleet command that could potentially have save the lives of countless millions for the good of the few.

It is nevertheless that the star trek universe is sadist in its core nature and propelling the sadist element of the star trek universe misled it's many fans to embrace star trek's diverse stories of conflict and false sense of self-actualization. In truth one is to see star trek in light of the reality of conflict. That conflict is not to be desired or embraced but to be avoided at all cost. That war is not to be encouraged and glorified. A war-like society, as the star trek universe, is a society that is constantly at war and strives to encourage and instigate conflict in order to achieve further societal development and fulfillment. Within only a matter of months a society that is constantly at war will be, in all likely, wiped out. And for those reasons the longevity of the star trek universe is short-live.